an infatuations notebook

Baseball

by Vincent Scilla

M·Q·P

Baseball is a team game with a strong focus on the individual. It allows the individual to shine and succeed as part of the team. The fans can identify with their heroes and ride the highs and lows of their team's forever changing fortunes, thus feeling a strong connection and attachment that will last a lifetime.

Notes

As an artist and former ballplayer in my youth, I've made that bond with baseball. What fascinated me as a boy were the picture cards of ball players from Brooklyn, Chicago, New York and Cincinnati posed against the advertising backdrops of their ballparks.

 Notes

Baseball was, is and always will be to me the best game in the world.

Babe Ruth (1895–1948), N.Y. Yankees outfielder (1920–34)

The Babe (in retirement)

I built my own imaginary ballpark from my erector set and pasted my own advertisements on the walls. Years later, I've taken this same passion to my painting – searching for the feel of those faraway places and the hope that some day I would see them.

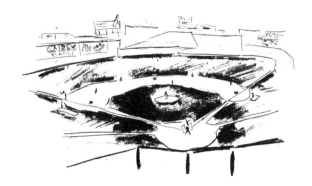

Notes

Next to religion, baseball has furnished a greater impact on American life than any other institution.

Herbert Hoover, thirty-first president of the United States

When I began playing the game, baseball was as gentlemanly as a kick in the crotch.

Ty Cobb (1886–1961), Detroit Tigers outfielder (1905–26)

In one of baseball's earliest forms, called 'townball', the field was square with no foul lines and a single out retired the side. The 'striker' was out if the ball was caught in the air or if the runner was 'soaked' – hit with the ball before reaching base.

Princeton College banned this game of townball in 1787 as "low and unbecoming of gentlemen students". On the other hand, Henry Wadsworth Longfellow found that ballplaying "communicated such an impulse to our limbs and joints that there is nothing now heard of in our leisure hours, but ball, ball, ball. I cannot prophesy with any degree of accuracy concerning the continuance of this rage for play, but the effect is good, since there has been a thoroughgoing reformation from inactivity and turpitude."

I see great things in baseball. It's our game – the American game. It will take our people out-of-doors, fill them with oxygen, give them a larger physical stoicism. Tend to relieve us from being a nervous, dyspeptic set. Repair these losses, and be a blessing to us.

Walt Whitman, poet and journalist

Walter Johnson

Notes

Contemporary Account of Baseball, in the 1830s: "The first day the Philadelphia men took the field … only four men were found to play, so they started in by playing a game called 'Catball'. All the players were over twenty-five years of age, and to see them playing a game like this caused much merriment among the friends of the players. It required 'sand' in those days to go out on the field and play, as the prejudice against the game was very great. It took nearly a whole season to get men enough together to make a team, owing to the ridicule heaped upon the players for taking part in such childish sports."

Notes

Notes

The baseball bat is made from white ash. Although it weighs less than the cricketer's bat (30–36 ounces to 40–50 ounces), it feels heavier because it is held at shoulder height. It measures just 9 inches in circumference. The ball, with a weight of nearly 5 ounces, is made with a cork center that is wound with woolen yarn and covered with two pieces of cowhide that is stitched precisely 216 times.

The Pitchers Hand

Baseball has no penalties at all. A home run is a home run. You cheer. In football, on a score, you look for flags. If there's one, who's it on? When can we cheer? Football acts can be repealed. Baseball acts stand forever.

Thomas Boswell, author

There are only five things you can do in baseball –
run, throw, catch, hit and hit with power.

Leo Durocher (1905–94) baseball executive (1939–73)

On September 23, 1845 Alexander Cartwright and twenty-eight other young men formed the New York Knickerbocker Baseball Club in New York City. Cartwright, with the help of Daniel Lucius 'Doc' Adams of New Hampshire, would draw up a set of rules that defined the game as we know it today.

The rules

The playfield would be a diamond with bases set forty-two paces apart. The ball would be pitched under-hand with a straight wrist and elbow delivery. Foul lines were established, the batter received three missed swings before being called out and, perhaps for safety reasons, the runner was to be tagged or thrown out, not thrown at.

On June 19, 1846, on the Elysian fields of Hoboken, New Jersey the first game played under these new rules was held. The New York Baseball Ball Club defeated Cartwright and his Knickerbockers twenty-three to one.

Alexander Joy Cartwright (center),
Founder of Baseball

Notes

Baseball is the very symbol, the outward and visible expression of the drive and push and rush and struggle of the raging, tearing, booming nineteenth century.

Mark Twain, author

Notes

The New York game was spreading throughout the Northeast to Maine and west to Oregon and California when it was interrupted by the Civil War in 1861. The war, however, further established baseball as America's game, one reason being the great portability of the game and the fact that the field required little maintenance, say, compared to a cricket pitch. Soldiers in both armies quickly took to the game in prison yards and battlefields.

B aseball soon became a business. In 1869 the first professional team took the field – the Cincinnati Red Stockings. They were managed by Harry Wright, the British-born son of a professional cricketer. Their first season was a success, with a record of sixty-five victories and no losses. They made a profit of $1.39. George Wright, Harry's younger brother, was paid the hefty sum of $1400, for playing on the team.

My high salary for one season was forty-six thousand dollars and a Cadillac. If I were to get paid a million, I'd feel that I should sweep out the stadium every night after I finished playing the game.

Duke Snider (1926–), Brooklyn Dodgers outfielder (1947–57)

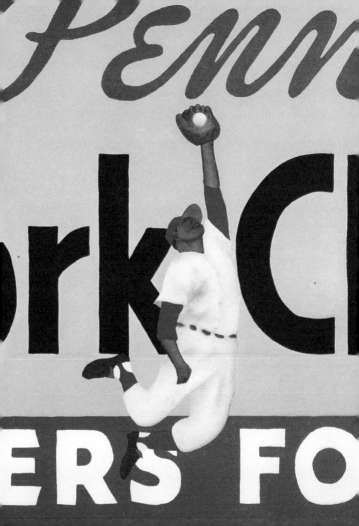

Horace Wilson, a professor in Tokyo during the 1870s, is credited as being the Abner Doubleday of Japan, teaching baseball to his students. Beisuboru, as it came to be called, began to take a slow but steady grip on the Japanese imagination. By 1930 beisuboru rivaled sumo as the national pastime.

Many visits by American baseball stars, such as Ty Cobb, Babe Ruth, Lou Gehrig and Lefty Grove, greatly increased the popularity of the game. After World War II Japanese professional leagues, the Central and Pacific, began the Japan Series to crown their national champion. Sadaharu Oh, with his Mel Ott style leg kick, became the home run king of Japan with 868, during a career begun in the late 1950s.

Just as the Japanese have embraced baseball with a fanatical fervor, the people of Latin America and the Caribbean have done much the same. Baseball first gained a foothold in Cuba during the 1870s; from there it spread to the Dominican Republic, Puerto Rico and on to Venezuela and Mexico, and throughout the Latin American world. It was during the 1950s that stars such as Roberto Clemente, Orlando Cepeda and Luis Aparicio showcased the talent and style of the Hispanic ballplayer; a style that is very much a part of the tradition of professional baseball that is played today.

Casey at the Bat

The sneer is gone from Casey's lip;
His teeth are clenched in hate;
He pounds with cruel violence
  his bat upon the plate
And now the pitcher holds the ball,
  and now he lets it go
And now the air is shattered
  by the force of Casey's blow

Oh! somewhere in this favored land
  the sun is shining bright
The band is playing somewhere,
  and somewhere hearts are light
And somewhere men are laughing
  and somewhere children shout;
But there is no joy in Mudville –
  Mighty Casey has struck out.

Ernest L. Thayer – the last two stanzas of the poem – published
in the *San Francisco Examiner*, June 3, 1888

Oh, don't you remember the game of baseball,
we saw twenty years ago played,
When contests were true, and the sight free to all, and
home-runs in plenty were made?
When we lay on the grass, and with thrills of delight,
watched the ball squarely pitched at the bat,
And easily hit, and then mount out of sight
along with our cheers and our hat?
And then, while the fielders raced after the ball,
the men on the bases flew round,
And came in together – four batters in all.
Ah! That was the old game renowned.
Now salaried pitchers, who throw the ball curved
at padded and masked catchers lame
And gate money music and seats all reserved
is all is left of the game.

Oh, give us the glorious matches of old, when love of
true sport made them great,
And not this new-fashioned affair always sold for the
boodle they take at the gate.

H. C. Dodge
Yearning for the good ol' days – I guess (1886)

1900 Rules change: home plate is changed from a 12 inch square to a five-sided figure, 17 inches in width.

1901 Rules change: the National League rules that a foul ball not caught on the fly is counted as a strike unless the batter already has two strikes. The American League adopts the rule in 1903.

I couldn't see well enough to play when I was a boy, so they gave me a special job – they made me the umpire.

Harry S. Truman, thirty-third president of the United States

Ideally, the umpire should combine the integrity of a Supreme Court Justice, the physical agility of an acrobat, the endurance of Job, and the imperturbability of Buddha.

Anonymous

At 5'9", 165 lbs, Ray 'Cracker' Schalk (Cracker, because he looked like a box of crackers when he squatted behind the plate) was a catcher who couldn't hit but sure could catch – more than one hundred games 12 years in a row. That's a lot of service for a position that offers broken fingers, bruised shins and aching knees as a reward. Ray was the model for defensive catchers throwing out base-stealers like Cobb and expanding the catcher's duties to backing up first and third bases. Baseball is not all hitting and Ray proved this out.

1903 October 1, the first World Series between the American and National Leagues is played at Boston's Huntington Avenue Ground, featuring the Boston Pilgrims of the American League and the Pittsburgh Pirates from the National. The Pirates won the first game but Boston won the series five games to three.

Notes

Notes

You gotta be a man to play baseball for a living but you gotta have a lot of little boy in you, too.

Roy Campanella (1921–95),
Brooklyn Dodgers catcher (1948–57)

I wanted to be a big league baseball player so I could see my picture on a bubble gum card.

Al Ferrara (1939–), Los Angeles Dodgers outfielder (1963–68)

I don't know anything about ballet, but I wish people would watch baseball the way ballet fans watch the dance – not to see who wins but to see how well each player performs his part.

Mike Marshall (1943–), Los Angeles Dodgers pitcher (1974–6)

 Notes

It's the only occupation where a man has to be perfect the first day on the job and then improve over the years.

Ed Runge, current American League umpire

Ump says – safe and home

1904 The American and National Leagues increase their schedules from 140 to 154 games, which remained the standard until 1961, when the American added two new teams and increased its schedule to 162 games. The National followed the same program in 1962.

1908 Rules change: pitchers are prohibited from soiling or scruffing a new ball. A batter is credited with a sacrifice fly and not charged with a time at bat if he hits a fly ball that is caught, and a runner tags up and scores after the catch.

ilford

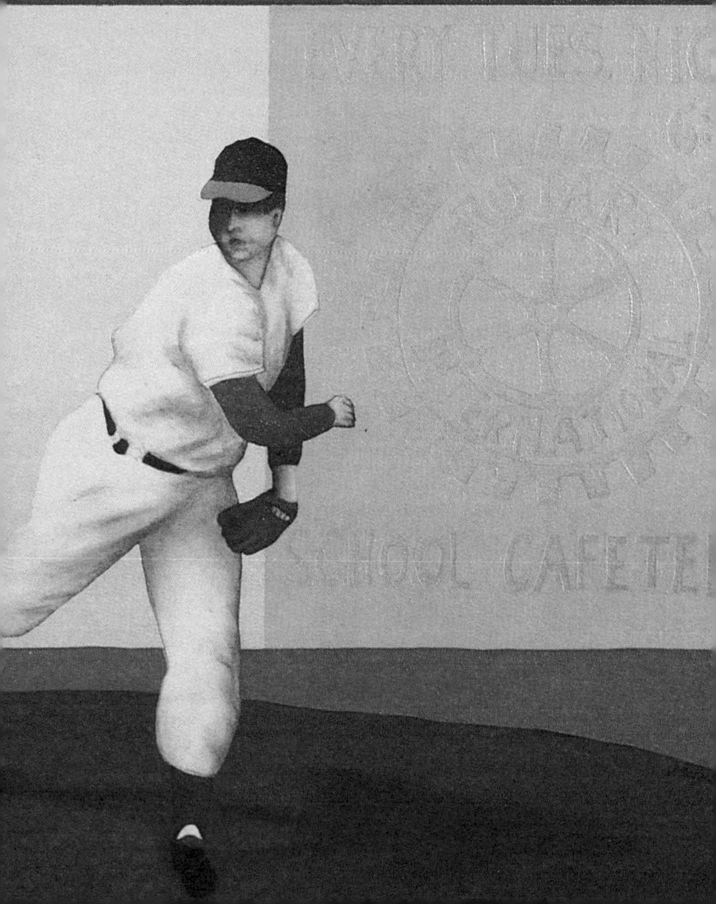

Take Me Out To The Ballgame (Song)

Take me out
to the ball game
Take me out
with the crowd.

Buy me some peanuts
and Cracker Jack,
I don't care if
I never get back,
Let me root, root, for the home team,
If they don't win it's a shame –

For it's one, two, three strikes you're out
At the old ball game.

Jack Norworth, vaudeville entertainer (1908).
Inspired by the advertisement '*Baseball Today – Polo Grounds*'
seen on an elevated Manhattan train

Notes

1908 Henry Chadwick, who published the first baseball guide book in 1860 and later ran *Spalding's Official Baseball Guide,* dies at age 83. His most famous contribution to the game may have been his development of the box score and his system of scoring, which are so necessary for this game of records. This serves as a compilation of statistics from each ballplayer on the team, keeping statistics on at bats, hits, errors and strikeouts for example.

Pitching is the art of instilling fear.

Sandy Koufax (1939–), Los Angeles Dodgers pitcher (1963–68)

The ball once struck off,
Away flies the boy
To the next destined post,
And then home with joy.

Anonymous

 Notes

Every day is a new opportunity. You can build on yesterday's success or put its failures behind and start over again. That's the way life is, with a new game every day, and that's the way baseball is.

Bob Feller, Cleveland Indians pitcher (1936–56)

Sain in the Rain
Johnny Sain, Boston Braves pitcher (1942–51)

There is magic in the moment. For when I open my eyes and see my sons in the place where my father once sat, I feel an invisible bond between our three generations, an anchor of loyalty linking my sons to the grandfather whose face they never saw but whose person they have already come to know through this most timeless of all sports, baseball.

Doris Kearns Goodwin, author

Baseball is continuous, like nothing else among American things, an endless game of repeated summers, joining the long generations of all the fathers and all the sons.

Donald Hall, poet

A hot dog at the ballpark is better than steak at the Ritz.

Humphrey Bogart, actor

1909 Rules change: a foul bunt – when the ball is hit in a certain way horizontally – with two strikes is a strikeout. A pitcher or catcher is charged with an error if a wild pitch or a passed ball on the third strike allows a batter to reach first base.

Notes

Though it is a team game by definition, it is actually a series of loosely connected individual efforts.

Bill Veeck, Chicago baseball executive (1959)

Baseball is like a poker game. Nobody wants to quit when he's losing; nobody wants you to quit when you're ahead.

Jackie Robinson, Brooklyn Dodgers infielder (1947–56)

These are the saddest of possible words–
   Tinker to Evers to Chance,
Trio of Bear Cubs and fleeter than birds–
   Tinker to Evers to Chance,
Thoughtlessly pricking our gonfalon bubble,
   Making a giant hit into a double,
Words that are weighty with nothing but
   trouble Tinkers to Evers to Chance

Franklin P. Adams, columnist, *New York Mail,* July 1910, writing about the Chicago Cubs double play combination – a play involving three fielders, in this case, shortstop Tinker, second base Evers and first base Chance.

1910 April 14 US President Willliam H. Taft becomes the first president to throw out the first ball of the season on opening day in Washington, D.C. His presence makes baseball the 'official' national pastime. Walter 'Big Train' Johnson pitches a one-hitter and the Washington Senators defeat the Philadelphia Athletics one to nothing.

Walter 'Big Train' Johnson, Washington Senators (1907–27)

Notes

1912 April 20 The Boston Red Sox play their first game at Fenway Park, Boston, where they still play today. The Detroit Tigers play their first game in reconstructed Bennett Park. The next year concrete stands are poured and the park is renamed Navin Field. Later it became Briggs Stadium and was renamed once again in 1961 as Tiger Stadium, the current home of the Detroit Tigers.

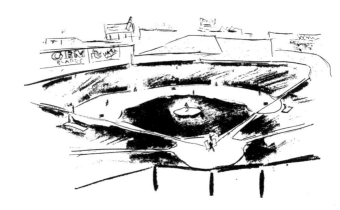

Day Game in Boston

Notes

No one can ever see the ball hit the bat because it's physically impossible to focus your eyes that way. However, when I hit especially hard, I could smell the leather start to burn as it struck the wooden bat.

Ted Williams (1918–), Boston Red Sox outfielder (1939–60)

Notes

1914 In July the Boston Red Sox purchase the contract of George Herman 'Babe' Ruth from Providence of the International League. The Babe's first contract paid one hundred dollars a month. As a nineteen year old pitcher he appears in five games and has a record of two wins and one loss.

When I was a small boy in Kansas, a friend of mine and I went fishing … I told him I wanted to be a real major league baseball player, a genuine professional like Honus Wagner. My friend said that he'd like to be president of the United States. Neither of us got our wish.

Dwight D Eisenhower, thirty-fourth president of the United States

1916 Fans at Chicago's Weegham Park, home of the Cubs, are allowed to keep any baseball hit into the stands. This proves to be such a popular fan policy that it is quickly adopted by many other teams. Today, this policy exists at virtually all levels of professional baseball.

All literary men are Red Sox fans – to be a Yankee far in a literate society is to endanger your life.

John Cheever, author

A critic once characterized baseball as six minutes of action crammed into two-and-one-half hours.

Ray Fitzgerald, sportswriter

Notes

You can shake a dozen glove men out of a tree, but the bat separates the men from the boys.

Dale Long (1926–), Washington Senators first baseman (1961–2)

Hands of the Batter

Baseball is something more than a game to an American boy; it is his training field for life work. Destroy his faith in its squareness and honesty and you have destroyed something more; you have planted suspicion of all things in his heart.

Judge Kenesaw Mountain Landis, baseball commissioner (1920–44)

Judge Kenesaw Mountain Landis

Notes

1919 October 9 The Cincinnati Reds defeat the heavily favored Chicago White Sox in the World Series by five games to three. Not until September of the next year would it be found out that eight members of the White Sox conspired with gamblers and fixed the outcome of the World Series. The faith of a nation had been compromised; baseball's first commissioner, Judge Kenesaw Mountain Landis, banned those eight from baseball for life.

A poor, uneducated country boy, 'shoeless' Joe Jackson swung his bat, 'Black Betsy', with such perfection that Babe Ruth adopted his swing and called it one of the best he had ever seen. Jackson's .356 career average is the third best ever. However, it was his association with gamblers and the fixing of the 1919 World Series for which he is remembered. Along with other players he was banned from major league baseball in 1920 as one of the 'eight men out'. "Say it ain't so, Joe", but it was.

Whether you want to or not, you do serve as a role model. People will always put more faith in baseball players than anyone else.

Brooks Robinson (1937–), Baltimore Orioles third baseman 1955-57)

1920 With efforts to integrate baseball having little success, Rube Foster, manager of the Chicago American Giants, brings together owners of other black baseball teams in Kansas City to form the Negro National League. Original League teams are the Chicago American Giants, Chicago Giants, Cuban Stars (based in Cincinnati), Detroit Stars, Kansas City Monarchs, St Louis Giants, Dayton Marcos and the Indianapolis ABCs.

1920 January 3 Boston Red Sox owner Harry Frazee, in need of cash and a loan to finance a Broadway Show, sells Babe Ruth to the New York Yankees for $125,000 in cash and a $300,000 personal loan from Colonel Jacob Ruppert, a New York brewer and Yankee owner. A curse has been on Boston since. However, Frazee did get a winner with 'No, no, Nanette'.

I swing big, with everything I've got. I hit big or I miss big. I like to live as big as I can.

Babe Ruth (1895–1948), N.Y. Yankees outfielder (1920–34)

The first big-league game I ever saw was at the Polo Grounds. My father took me. I remember it so well – the green grass and the green stands. It was like seeing Oz.

John Curtis (1948–), San Francisco Giants pitcher (1977–9)

1920 August 16 Carl Mays, pitching for the New York Yankees, hits Cleveland shortstop Ray Chapman in the head. Chapman is instantly knocked out and dies the next day without regaining consciousness. This is baseball's first – and only – on-the-field fatality.

Notes

1921 The first radio broadcast of a baseball game hits the airwaves in Pittsburgh at Radio Station KDKA. Harold Arlin is at the microphone. Baseball owners are skeptical of radio's effect on attendance and are slow to embrace baseball radio broadcasts. However, they decided against banning radio from the ballpark – a wise decision.

Baseball is the only game you can see on the radio.

Phil Hersh, sportswriter, *Chicago Tribune*

1923 After being asked (the previous year) to leave the Polo Grounds, which the New York Yankees shared with the New York Giants, Colonel Jacob Ruppert begins construction of Yankee Stadium across the river from the Polo Grounds in the Bronx, New York. Dubbed 'The house that Ruth built', the stadium opened on April 18 to a reported crowd of 74,000. The Yankees defeated the Red Sox with Babe Ruth hitting two home runs in a four to one victory.

The secret of managing is to keep the guys who hate you away from the guys who are undecided.

Casey Stengel (1889–1975) N.Y. Baseball executive (1949–65)

1925 Wally Pipp, the New York Yankee first baseman, begs out of the day's game lineup for June 2. He is replaced by Lou Gehrig, who plays the next 2130 consecutive games. An unfortunate time for a headache; Mr Pipp is sold to the Cincinnati Reds the next season.

Tyrus Raymond Cobb, 'the Georgia Peach', a savage base stealer, 4000 plus hit man (in the 1980s passed by another man of equal determination – Pete Rose) and the holder of the highest career batting average of .366, batted below .300 only during his rookie (first) year of 1905. He was a mainstay for the Detroit Tigers, retiring after two years in Philadelphia in 1928.

"We may never see his like again", Connie Mack said of Ty Cobb. A true prophesy.

Notes

1928 An idea that had been floating around for about twenty years is picked up by National League President John Heydler – the designated hitter. The idea proposes that a hitter take the pitcher's turn in the batting order and thereby interject more offense into the game, making it "a better and livelier game". Fan opposition is so strong that the idea is quickly dropped. Forty-five years later, in 1973, the American League, with or without fan approval, was to adopt the designated hitter.

One of the chief duties of the fan is to engage in arguments with the man behind him. This department has been allowed to run down fearfully.

Robert Benchley, author

1931 March 3 'The Star Spangled Banner,' a song written by Francis Scott Key in 1814 during the War of 1812, is designated the United States National Anthem by the US Congress and President Herbert Hoover. The fans have been standing to this anthem every ball game since.

No baseball fan has to explain his mania to any other baseball fan. They are a fraternity. It is less easy, often it is hopeless, to try to explain it to anyone else. You grow technical, and you do not make sense. You grow sentimental, and you are deemed soft in the head. How, the benighted outsider asks you with no little condescension, can you grow sentimental about a cold-blooded professional sport?

John K. Hutchens, author

 Notes

1932 October 1 Babe Ruth's 'called shot' home run off
Chicago Cubs pitcher Charlie Root helps the New York
Yankees to a seven to five victory in game three of the
World Series. The Babe took two pitches for strike and
motioned with his hand toward the outfield – deep
centerfield. This is exactly where the next pitch went
and the four to four tie and ballgame with it.

Ruthian mythology took another giant step forward.
It was also the Babe's last World Series homer.

Frank 'Home Run' Baker, Philadelphia Athletics & N.Y. Yankees
(1908–22)

The whole history of baseball has the quality of mythology.

Bernard Malamud, author

Basketball, hockey, and track meets are action heaped upon action, climax upon climax, until the onlooker's responses become deadened. Baseball is for the leisurely afternoons of summer and for the unchanging dreams.

Roger Kahn, author

1933 Acting upon a proposal by *Chicago Tribune* sports editor, Arch Ward, and based on an idea first put forth by sportswriter Grantland Rice, baseball executives faced with sagging attendance due to the Depression stage the first mid-season All-Star Game. The game is held at packed Comiskey Park between stars from the National and American Leagues chosen by fans who enter votes for favorite players into the ballot box. Once again, Babe Ruth rises to the occasion and the American League wins the contest four to two on a two-run homer by the aging star.

1935 The Cincinnati Reds play the first night game in the major leagues at Crosley Field in Cincinnati, Ohio. The idea was that of general manager Larry MacPhail, who had tried night baseball in the minor leagues. The Reds played seven home night games that year, every one a sellout. U.S. President Franklin D. Roosevelt pushed the button in the White House on May 24 and baseball said hello to the night.

1938 June 11 Johnny Vander Meer of the Cincinnati Reds tosses a three to nothing no-hitter over the Boston Braves in Cincinnati. On June 15, his next start, Vander Meer no-hits the Brooklyn Dodgers at their home park, Ebbets Field and also their first night game – I guess their excuse was they couldn't see the pitch.

Anyhow, it's off to Boston, where the Braves finally figure Vander Meer out and get a hit after three hitless plus innings. Two no-hitters in a row – hasn't been done since.

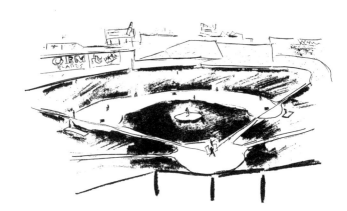

Notes

Whoever wants to know the heart and mind of America had better learn baseball, the rules and realities of the game – and do it by watching first some high school or small-town teams.

Jacques Barzun, author

1939 June 12 The Baseball Hall of Fame opens in the 'official' birthplace of baseball – Cooperstown, New York. Among those in attendance are previous inductees, Ty Cobb, Babe Ruth, Honus Wagner, Cy Young, as well as other living members of the Hall elected in the years 1936 through 1939.

Baseball is too much a business to them now. I loved baseball. I ate and slept it. But now the players, instead of picking up the sports page, pick up the *Wall Street Journal.* It's different.

Satchel Paige, Negro League pitcher (1926–47)

Lou Gehrig played in the shadows of Babe Ruth. He wasn't a 'headline' guy like the Babe, just a hardworking first baseman who played in 2130 straight games. Gehrig hit for power – 493 home runs and averaged a career .340. Known as the 'iron horse', his engine began to run down as a life threatening disease – amyotrophic lateral sclerosis – caused him to retire July 4, 1939 at Yankee Stadium. His parting words to the packed house, "Today, I consider myself the luckiest man on the face of the earth", are some of the most memorable in baseball. He was inducted into the Hall of Fame in 1939, two years before his death in 1941.

'Gehrig's Farewell'

Notes

1939 Very primitive by today's standards, using only two cameras, the first baseball game (Major League) televised from Ebbets Field in Brooklyn, New York. Red Barber calls the action for Radio Station WZXBS as the Dodgers lose to the Cincinnati Reds five to two. There are only four hundred or so television sets in New York City – a very exclusive viewing audience.

I don't think we had the pressures then that ballplayers have now, because there was no television.

Ralph Kiner, television announcer

1940 April 16 On Opening Day, the first game of the year, Bob Feller throws baseball's only Opening Day no-hitter to date.

Good pitching will always stop good hitting and vice-versa.

Casey Stengel (1889–1975), N.Y. baseball executive (1949–65)

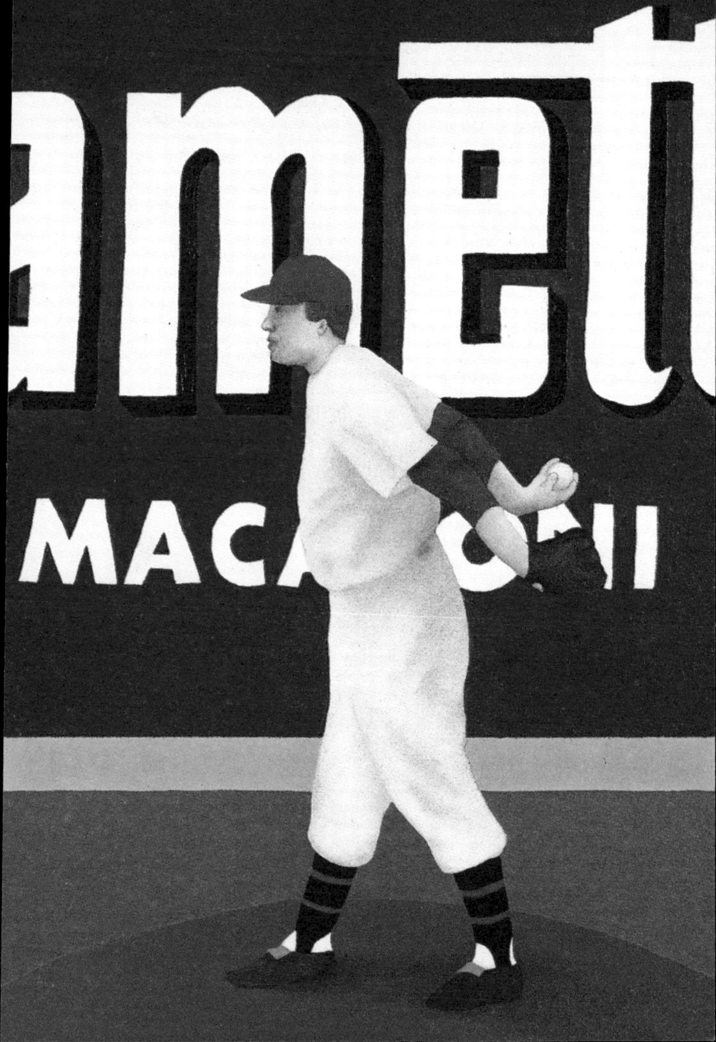

Ted Williams of the Boston Red Sox bats .406, hits 37 home runs and bats in 120 runs. However, he does not win the American League Most Valuable Player award; the award goes to Joe Dimaggio of the New York Yankees. Dimaggio leads the Yanks to the American League pennant, bats .357 with 30 homers and 125 runs batted in. It is his 56-game hitting streak, a record that still stands, that places him among baseball's greats.

Ted & Joe
Ted Williams, Boston Red Sox outfielder (1939–60) and
Joe Dimaggio, N.Y. Yankees outfielder (1936–51)

You always get a special kick on opening day, no matter how many you go through. You look forward to it like a birthday party when you're a kid. You think something wonderful is going to happen.

Joe Dimaggio (1914–), N.Y. Yankees outfielder (1936–51)

1942 Shortly after his death in 1941, *Pride of the Yankees*, a movie about the life of Lou Gehrig, opens. Gary Cooper plays Lou Gehrig. Babe Ruth and Bill Dickey, among other real sports figures, make guest appearances; and, of course, don't forget Walter Brennan, the great Hollywood character actor, in his role as a sportswriter.

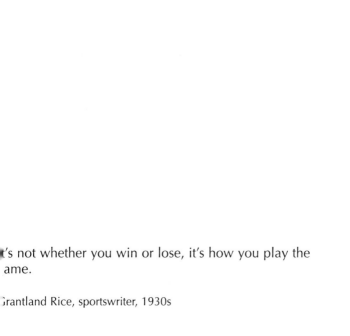

’s not whether you win or lose, it’s how you play the ame.

Grantland Rice, sportswriter, 1930s

Too old to be drafted and no longer the hitter he was, Jimme Fox found a war-time job in 1943: baseball manager. (Tom Hanks later found a similar job in the film *A League of Their Own*.) Founded by the chewing gum king, Philip Wrigley, the All-American Girls Baseball League recruited the best there was. However, "No pants-wearing, tough talkin' female softballer will play on any of our teams," Wrigley said. Looks and talent made the team.

Joanne Weaver had the ingredients, hitting .429 one season and winning three batting titles. The end of World War II began the demise of this successful league as the GIs returned home. The league closed in 1954.

Notes

I don't want to play golf. When I hit a ball, I want someone else to go chase it.

Rogers Hornsby (1896–1963), St Louis Cardinals infielder (1915–26)

The romance of baseball … is in its capacity for stirring fantasy. We are never too old or too bothered to see ourselves wrapping up a World Series victory with a homer in the final inning of the seventh game.

Ron Fimrite, author

Ernie's Seven Ball Trick
Ernie Lombardi, Cincinnati Reds catcher (1932–41)

Ernie "Schnozz" Lombardi was a big muscular guy, with a banana nose, an easy-going manner and feet of one hundred percent pure lead. However, his speed did not keep him from two batting titles: .342 in 1930 and .330 in 1943. He also caught Johnny Vander Meer's consecutive no-hitters.

1944 The St Louis Browns, perhaps benefiting from the fact that many of the top talent possessed by their rivals were currently serving military duty in the War, finish in first place in the American League. This is only their second finish over .500 in the previous fourteen years. They played their hometown rival, the St Louis Cardinals of the National League, and lost the World Series four games to two.

Baseball is almost the only orderly thing in a very unorderly world. If you get three strikes, even the best lawyer in the world can't get you off.

Bill Veeck, Chigaco White Sox owner (1959)

1945 October 23 Branch Rickey, general manager of the Brooklyn Dodgers, signs Jackie Roosevelt Robinson of the Negro League Kansas City Monarchs to a minor league contract with the Montreal Royals of the International League. After tearing up the League in 1946, Robinson joined the Dodgers in 1947, became Rookie of the Year and opened the doors of baseball to all.

The first black player before Jackie Robinson was Moses Fleetwood Walker, also a college man like Robinson, with Toledo of the American Association in 1884. However, a color line was drawn in 1887, which stood until sixty years later when Robinson broke it.

"Prince Hal" Newhouser, somewhat wrongly considered a wartime wonder during World War II when virtually all the stars were seeing military duty, quickly dispelled that belief by winning 26 and losing just 9 games in post-war America, 1946. Ted Williams of the Red Sox named him as one of the toughest pitchers to hit.

Hal Newhouser, Detroit Tigers pitcher (1939–53)

Notes

1947 Once again and continuing to the present day, baseball fans are given the opportunity to select the starting lineup for both teams – the American League and the National League, in the All-Star Game, by voting. This power was briefly given to the managers after the initial game in 1933. As John Lennon would have said, "Power to the people, right on!"

Poets are like baseball pitchers. Both have their
moments. The intervals are the tough things.

Robert Frost, poet

Your bat is your life. It's your weapon. You don't want to go into battle with anything that feels less than perfect.

Lou Brock (1939–), St Louis Cardinals outfielder (1964–79)

I was never nervous when I had the ball, but when I let it go I was scared to death.

Lefty Gomez, N.Y, Yankee pitcher (1930–42)

Supposedly, Galvin picked up the nickname 'Pud' for making 'pudding' out of the opposing batters. However, later in his career he did balloon up from his check-in weight of 190 pounds to a jiggly 320.

He was the greatest fat pitcher; his record will bear that out, along with his plaque at the Baseball Hall of Fame.

'Pud' Galvin, pitcher on various teams in the
National League (1875–92)

Notes

1948 With the integration of black ballplayers into both leagues, the American followed the National shortly after Jackie Robinson joined the Dodgers with Larry Doby joining the Chicago White Sox; the glory days of the Negro League were becoming a thing of the past. On October 5, the Washington Homestead Grays defeat the Birmingham Black Barons in the final Colored World Series.

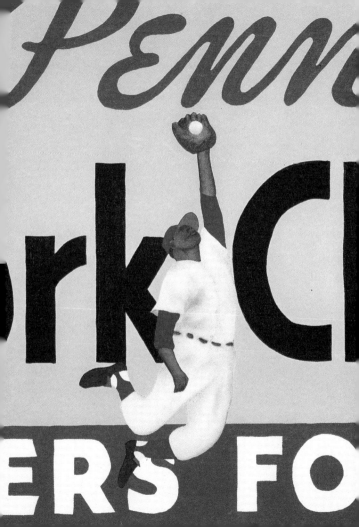

1949 Eddie Waitkus, the inspiration for the Bernard Malamud book *The Natural*, is shot in the chest by a female fan in her room at the Edgewater Beach Hotel in Chicago. He missed death and the rest of the season, returning in 1950 to help the Philadelphia Phillie 'Wiz Kids' to the World Series.

Spring is the time of year when the ground thaws, trees bud, the income tax falls due – and everyone wins the pennant.

Jim Murray, sportswriter, *Los Angeles Times*

Notes

Going to bed with a woman never hurt a ball player.
It's staying up all night looking for them that does you
in.

Casey Stengel (1889–1975), N.Y. baseball executive (1949–65)

Casey's Crystal Ball

1951 The Topps Company, the leading name and manufacturer of baseball cards, introduces its first series of cards with caramel candy, not bubblegum, included in the package. Don't worry – bubblegum soon followed and remained there until a few years ago, at which time I lost interest in buying cards with *no* gum.

The Jones of Baseball
share a name and a game ...

Pitchers: Cowboy Jones, Alex Jones, Al Jones, Barry Jones, Deacon Jones, Bumpus Jones, Charley Jones, Dale Jones, Jack Jones, Dick Jones, Doug Jones, Earl Jones, Elijah Jones, Gary Jones, Gordon Jones, Henry Jones, Jimmy Jones, Jim Jones, Jeff Jones, Broadway Jones, Ken Jones, Mike Jones, Mike C. Jones, Udell Jones, Oscar Jones, Percy Jones, Randy Jones, Sam Jones, Sam P. Jones, Sheldon Jones, Sherman Jones, Steve Jones, Rick Jones, Tim Jones.

Batters: Charlie Jones, Charlie F. Jones, Charley Jones, Chris Jones, Clarence Jones, Cleon Jones, Cobe Jones, Darryl Jones, Davy Jones, Fielder Jones, Frank Jones, Deacon Jones, Hal Jones, Henry Jones, Howie Jones, Dalton Jones, Jake Jones, Jeff Jones, Binky Jones, John Jones, Lynn Jones, Mack Jones, Red Jones, Ricky Jones, Bob Jones, Bob W. Jones, Ron Jones, Ruppert Jones, Jack Jones, Tracy Jones, Nippy Jones, Bill Jones, Bill D. Jones, Tex Jones, Tim Jones, Willie Jones.

1951 "The Giants win the Pennant, the Giants win the Pennant …" So said Russ Hodges as Bobby Thomson hit the "shot heard 'round the world" off Brooklyn's Ralph Branca on October 3. The New York Giants won the three-game playoff but lost the World Series to the New York Yankies. The 'shot' – it was a three-run homer.

A team is where a boy can prove his courage on his own. A gang is where a coward goes to hide.

Mickey Mantle (1931–1995), N.Y. Yankees outfielder (1951–68)

1953 October 5 As in four previous Octobers, the New York Yankees win the World Series – that's five in a row, sports fans, for the Yankee dynasty. Casey Stengel, the Yanks manager, has such an easy job just filling the names on the daily lineup card.

1954 You don't have to watch out for that sleeping glove anymore. Rules change: the custom of players leaving their gloves on the field at their positions is no longer permitted. Also, no throwing the glove at a batted ball: that'll cost you three bases.

1956 Once again it's October in New York with the Yankees. Once again the Yanks abuse those fall-guys from Brooklyn as Don Larsen pitches a perfect no runs, no hits, no errors baseball game. Need we ask who won the World Series?

Luther 'Dummy' Taylor (1875–1958),
N.Y. Giants pitcher (1900–08)

1955 A little too late for Ray Chapman; the batting helmet is made mandatory equipment in the National League. The American also follows the 'senior circuit' in 1956. Branch Rickey, now general manager for the Pittsburgh Pirates, is the source behind this sanity and Brooklyn finally wins the World Series!

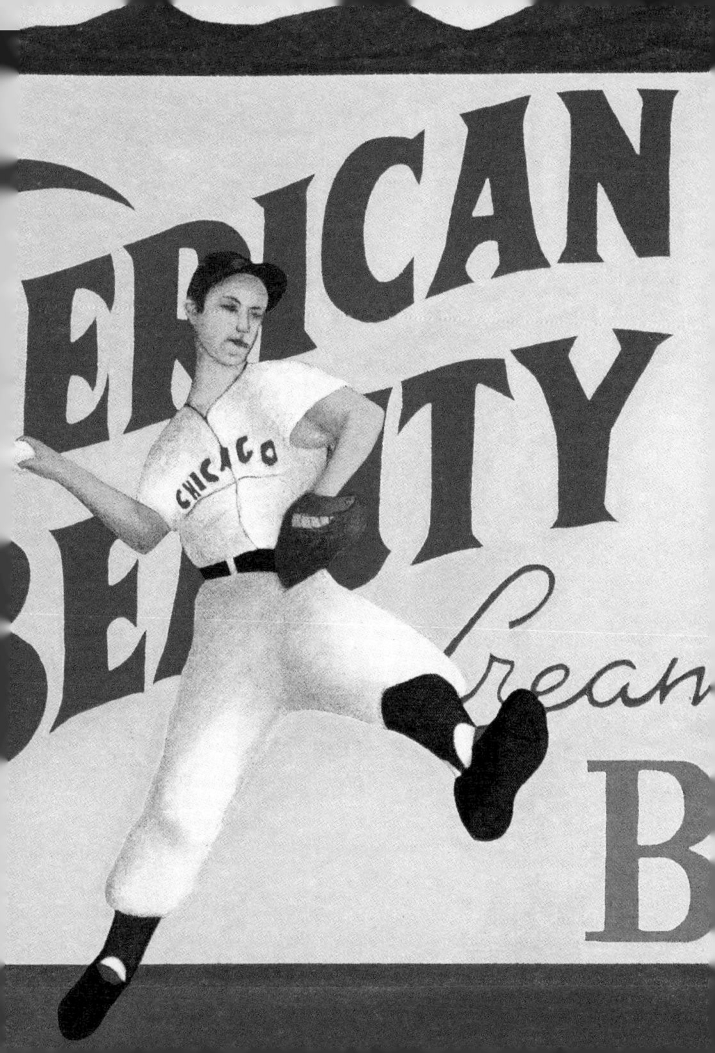
CHICAGO

This is really more fun than being president. I really do love baseball and I wish we could do this on the lawn every day. I wouldn't even complain if a stray ball came through the Oval Office window now and then.

Ronald Reagan, fortieth president of the United States

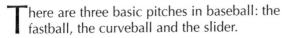

There are three basic pitches in baseball: the fastball, the curveball and the slider.

 Notes

The Pittsburgh Pirates are also known as the Bucs (derived from buccaneers).

Mr. Branch Rickey, baseball executive

I find baseball fascinating … Next to a triple play, baseball's double play is the most exciting and graceful thing in sports.

Alistair Cooke, journalist

"Mathewson warms up"
Christy Mathewson, N.Y. Giants pitcher (1900–16)

Notes

Baseball is all clean lines and clear decisions ... wouldn't life be far easier if it consisted of a series of definitive calls; safe or out, fair or foul, strike or ball. Oh, for a life like that, where every day produces a clear winner and an equally clear loser, and back to it the next day with the slate wiped clean and the teams starting out equal.

Eric Rolfe Greenberg, author

One thing I do well is hit fly balls. There's nothing quite like being able to hit towering flies. It's not like writing Beethoven's Ninth, but its definitely in the top two.

Charles Schulz, cartoonist

 Notes

he last time Willie Mays dropped a pop fly he had a
attle in one hand and bonnet on his head.

m Murray, sportswriter, *Los Angeles Times*

Willie Mays, N.Y. Giants outfielder (1951–57)

I believe managing is like holding a dove in your hand. If you hold it too tightly you kill it, but if you hold it too loosely, you lose it.

Tommy Lasorda (1927–), Los Angeles Dodgers manager

1957 Can we trust those fans to vote with their heads and not their hearts? In Cincinnati, I guess not. The fans vote in home players at seven of eight starting positions. Now, that is called stuffing the ballot box! Once again, the fans' vote is taken away by the Commissioner and given back to the players, managers and coaches.

Notes

A ballplayer has two reputations, one with the other players and one with the fans. The first is based on ability. The second the newspapers give him.

Johnny Evers (1883–1947), Chicago Cubs infielder (1902–13)

Son of Johnny Evers

Notes

The ever likable and popular Ernie Banks hit more home runs than any other shortstop, with 47 in 1958. He's also the first National Leaguer to win back-to-back Most Valuable Player awards. His sunny disposition and personal refrain of "Let's play two" made 'Mr Cub' a favorite of the Wrigley Field bleacher bums throughout his entire career spent with the Chicago Cubs.

Ernie's day to play to two
Ernie Banks, Chicago Cubs shortstop (1953–71)

Notes

I don't like to sound egotistical, but every time I stepped to the plate with a bat in my hands, I couldn't help but feel sorry for the pitcher.

Rogers Hornsby (1896–1963), St Louis Cardinals infielder (1915-26)

The Smiths of Baseball Has the name become an inspiration for the game?

Batters: Al Smith, Tony Smith, Klondike Smith, Billy Smith, Bobby Gene Smith, Brick Smith, Bernie Smith, Reggie Smith, Charlie Smith, Pop Smith, Charley Smith, Chris Smith, Earl Smith, Earl L. Smith, Edgar Smith, Mayo Smith, Mike Smith, Elmer Smith, Mike E. Smith, Carr Smith, Ernie Smith, Frank Smith, George Smith, Heine Smith …

… Red Smith, Milt Smith, Nate Smith, Ollie Smith, Ozzie Smith, Keith Smith, Paul Smith, Paul S. Smith, Dick Smith, Dick H. Smith, Dick K. Smith, Red P. Smith, Bob Smith, Joe Smith, Skyrocket Smith, Syd Smith, Tom Smith, Tommy Smith, Vinnie Smith, Wally Smith, Wib Smith, Red W. Smith, Bill Smith, Bill J. Smith, Willie Smith.

The Smiths of Baseball and the list goes on!
Pitchers: A. J. Smith, A. K. Smith, Art Smith, Billy Smith, Bryn Smith, Charlie Smith, Pop Smith, Pop-boy Smith, Clay Smith, Dave Smith, Dave S. Smith, Dave W. Smith, Doug Smith, Eddie Smith, Edgar Smith, Frank Smith, Frank T. Smith, Fred Smith, George Smith, Heine Smith, Germany Smith, George Smith, Hal Smith, Harry Smith ...

… Jack Smith, Jake Smith, Phenomenal Smith, Chick Smith, Lee Smith, Roy Smith, Mark Smith, Mike E. Smith, Mike A. Smith, Pete Smith, Pete L. Smith, Reggie Smith, Ed Smith, Bob Smith, Bob R. Smith, Bob R. G. Smith, Bob R. W. Smith, Rufus Smith, Sherry Smith, Tom Smith, Bill E. Smith, Bill W. Smith, Willie Smith, Zane Smith.

1960 was a year of a couple of dramatic finishes. The first being the career of Ted Williams, which ended with his 521st home run on his last at bat with the Boston Red Sox. Despite the urgent pleas of fans and fellow teammates – even the umpires – Ted would not take a bow as he had never done this during his entire career. It was Ted's way.

No game in the world is as tidy and dramatically neat as baseball, with cause and effect, crime and punishment, motive and result, so cleanly defined.

Paul Gallico, author

The second dramatic finish of 1960 was Bill Mazeroski's game ending home run for the Pittsburgh Pirates in game seven of the World Series versus the New York Yankees. The game also turned out to be Casey 'the old professor' Stengel's last for the Yankees, as their manager. He found employment with 'Amazin' New York Mets the next year.

Hack Wilson, Chicago Cubs outfielder (1926–31)

If you're not having fun in baseball, you miss the point of everything.

Chris Chambliss (1948–), Atlanta Braves first baseman (1980–86)

1961 was a tough year for the Babe. Roger Maris of the New York Yankees hit sixty-one home runs to break Babe Ruth's previous record of sixty, set in 1927 with the same New York Yankees.

Every day in every way, baseball gets fancier. A few more years and they'll be playing on oriental rugs.

Russell Baker, columnist, *New York Times*

The 1960s was a decade of great pitchers such as Gibson, Drysdale and Marichal. It was Sandy Koufax who defined them all. In a period from 1962 to the end of the 1966 season, Koufax won five ERA titles, pitched four no-hitters and won the CY Young Award, three times as the most outstanding pitcher in both the National and American Leagues. Casey Stengel wasn't wrong when he said, "The Jewish kid is probably the best of them".

Notes

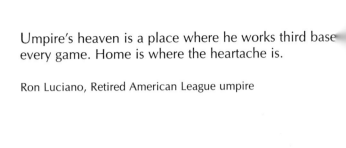

Umpire's heaven is a place where he works third base every game. Home is where the heartache is.

Ron Luciano, Retired American League umpire

The space between the white lines – that's my office. That's where I conduct my business.

Early Wynn, Cleveland Indians pitcher (1949–57)

Baseball? It's just a game – as simple as a ball and bat. Yet, complex as the American spirit it symbolizes. It's a sport, business – and sometimes even religion.

Ernie Harwall, broadcaster, Detroit Tigers, since the 1950s

A baseball club is part of the chemistry of the city. A game isn't just an athletic contest. It's a picnic, a kind of town meeting.

Michael Burke, N.Y. Yankees president

Notes

In 1972 Roberto Clemente of the Pittsburgh Pirates collected his 3000th hit on his final at bat of the season. Ten weeks later tragedy struck as Clemente's plane loaded with relief supplies for the earthquake victims of Nicaragua crashed into the sea on New Year's Eve. His body was never found. Shortly after his death Roberto Clemente was enshrined in the Baseball Hall of Fame – the first Latin American ballplayer to be inducted.

974 was a great year for the Oakland Athletics, who won their third consecutive World Series. The only other team to achieve this is not surprisingly the New York Yankees, who did it five times in a row from 1949 to 1953. The Yanks, by the way, are once again World Champions in 1996.

1974 was another tough year for the Babe. On April 8, Hank Aaron of the Atlanta Braves would homer off Al Downing for home run number 715, breaking Babe Ruth's career home run total. Hank would further advance the mark to 755 home runs before retiring in 1976.

Baseball gives you every chance to be great. Then it puts the pressure on you to prove that you haven't got what it takes. It never takes away the chance, and it never eases up on the pressure.

Joe Garagiola, St Louis Cardinals catcher (1946–51)

Josh Gibson, Homestead Gray–Negro League catcher
(1929–47)

These moments are the soul of baseball; the ball perfectly hit, perfectly caught, or perfectly thrown … We can unwrap the moments later, when it's quiet, and enjoy them all over again.

Alison Gordon, author

Notes

On the evening of September 11, 1985 hometown boy Pete Rose broke Ty Cobb's career hit record of 4191 before an adoring Cincinnati crowd. Rose would end his career with a total of 4256 hits.

To compare baseball with other team games is to say the Hope Diamond is a nice chunk of carbon. The endless variety of physical and mental skill demanded by baseball is both uncomparable and incomparable.

Bill Veeck, Chicago White Sox owner (1959)

When you get on first, know you are going to second. Know you can beat the pitcher and the catcher and the two of them combined. You have to have an inner conceit to be a successful base stealer. You have to know you are better than either the pitcher or the catcher.

Peter Reiser (1919–81), Brooklyn Dodgers outfielder (1940–8)

In 1988 the Los Angeles Dodgers faced a mighty opponent in the Oakland Athletics in that fall's World Series. In the first game with the Athletics leading four to three with two out in the bottom of the ninth, Kirk Gibson hobbled to the plate. Effectively unable to run due to various leg injuries, Gibson went to the plate looking for one good swing. Dennis Eckersley, the best relief pitcher in baseball, quickly got the count to three balls and two strikes. His pitch number six will long be remembered as Gibson launched it ten rows deep into the bleachers – the Dodgers win!

Pitching is just an illusion. You're dealing with a man's eyes. Make him think he's getting one thing and give him another and you've got him.

Ted Williams (1918–), Boston Red Sox outfielder (1939–60)

In 1989, nineteen year old Ken Griffey Jr. joined the Seattle Marineers. His father was playing with the Cincinnati Reds, making them the first father and son to play major league baseball of the same time. The following year Dad joined Junior as a member of the Seattle team. They even hit back to back homers – another first. Today, Ken Griffey Jr. is perhaps the best player playing. He can do it all – hit, hit for power, run, catch and throw.

If great teams are measured by World Series victories then the Atlanta Braves have some work left. As of 1996 the Braves have gone to the Autumn Classic four times during the 90s. They have, however, only won one time, a record not befitting such a fine team.

Al Lopez, National Leaguer (1928–47)

Notes

It's pitching, hitting, and defense that wins. Any two can win. Any three make you unbeatable.

Joe Garagiola, St Louis Cardinals catcher (1946–51)

You can't hit what you can't see.

Walter Johnson (1887–1946), Washington Senators pitcher,
(1907–27) describing his pitching strategy

The only real happiness a ballplayer has is when he is playing a ball game and accomplishes something he didn't think he could do.

Ring Lardner, author

Notes

Hideo Nomo, formerly of the Kintetsu Buffaloes, a professional baseball team in Japan, joined the Los Angeles Dodgers in 1995. He quickly became a national and international sensation with his unique pitching motion and live fast ball.

The people of Japan would be awake at all odd hours watching live television broadcasts of the national hero pitching in the United States. He was named the National League Rookie of the Year and has established himself as the first Japanese star in American baseball.

A very good team from Canada, the Toronto Blue Jays, have won the World Series twice – 1992 and 1993. Their victories have made baseball truly an international sport.

William Shakespeare on baseball:

"Why these balls bound" – *The Merry Wives of Windsor*

"Now, Let's have a catch" – *Twelfth Night*

"And so I shall catch the fly" – *Henry V*

"You base ballplayers" – *King Lear*

"As swift in motion as a ball" – *Romeo and Juliet*

"Have you scored me?" – *Othello*
"He proved best man i' the field" – *Coriolanus*
"What foul play had we" – *The Tempest*
"These nine men in buckram" – *Henry VI*
"Let us see you in the field" – *Troilus and Cressida*
"What works, my countrymen, in hand?
  Where go you with bats and clubs?" – *Coriolanus*

The good Lord was kind to me. He gave me a strong body, a good right arm, and a weak mind.

Dizzy Dean, St Louis Cardinals pitcher (1930–37)

Nicknames in baseball:

'Fidgety' Phil Collins
'Pretzels' Pezzullo – John Pezzullo
'Twitchy' Dick Pouter – Richard Pouter
'Jumping' Jack Jones
'Herky Jerky' Horton – Elmer Horton
'Dixie' Walker – Ewart Walker
'Texas' Jack Kraus
'Rebel' Oakes – Ennis Oakes
'Broadway' Jones – Kenneth Jones
'Cannonball' Crane – Edward Crane
'Smokey' Joe Wood
'Scooter' Rizzuto – Phil Rizzuto
'Deerfoot' Harry Bay

Notes

Harry 'the Cat' Breecher
'Pea Ridge' Day – Clyde Day
'Vinegar Bend' Mizell – Wilmer Mizell
'Jitter' Joe Berry
'Sad' Sam Jones
'Sunny' Jim Bottomley
'Bugs' Raymond – Arthur Raymond
'Scrappy' Bill Joyce
'Smiling' Mickey Welch
'Sweetbread' Bailey – Abraham Bailey
'Oyster' Burns – Thomas Burns
'Spud' Krist – Howard Krist
'Moose' McCormick – Harry McCormick
'Rabbit' Maranville – Walter Maranville
'Spider' Jorgensen – John Jorgensen
'Ducky' Medwick – Joe Medwick
'Hippo' Jim Vaughn
'Bubba' Church – Emory Church
'Dutch' Leonard – Emil Leonard
'Honest' John Kelly
George 'Catfish' Metkovich
Hollis 'Sloppy' Thurston

Trying to throw a fastball by Hank Aaron is like trying to sneak the sun past a rooster.

Curt Simmons (1929–), Philadelphia Phillies pitcher (1947–1960)

Notes

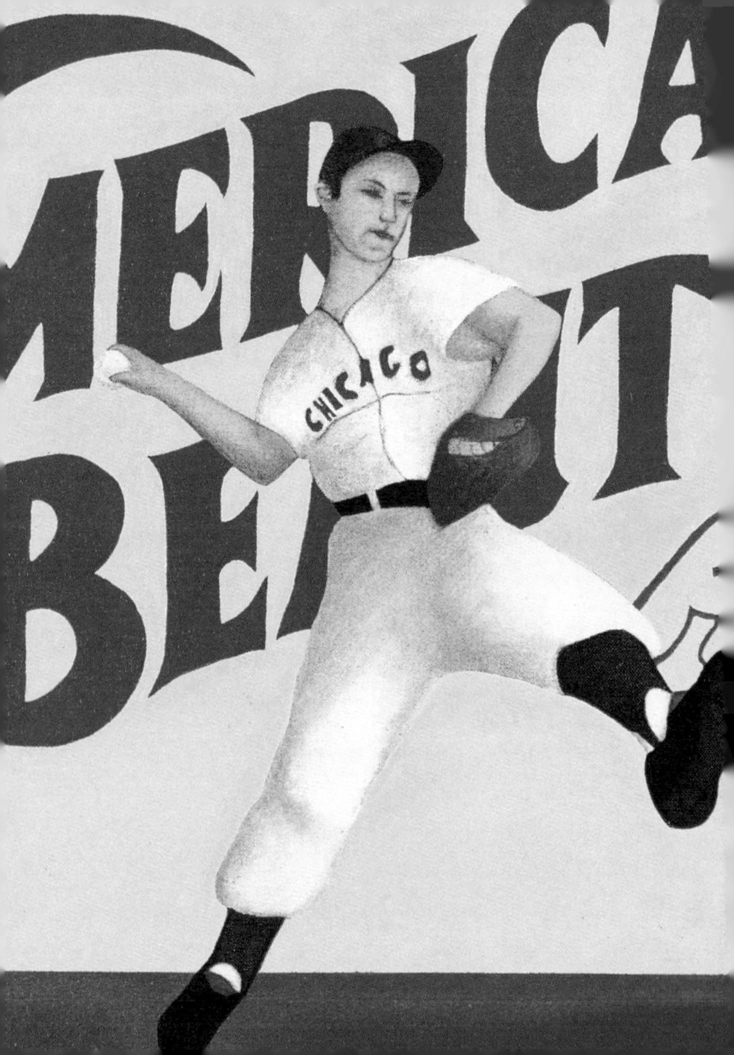
CHICAGO

mery

BUTT

V. Scha '85

The clock doesn't matter in baseball. Time stands still or moves backward. Theoretically, one game could go on forever. Some seem to.

Herb Caen, columnist, *San Francisco Chronicle*

Notes

Published by Museum Quilts Publications, Ltd.
254-258 Goswell Road, London EC1V 7EB

Copyright © Museum Quilts Publications, Ltd. 1997

Text © Vincent Scilla 1997
Illustrations © Vincent Scilla 1997

ISBN: 1-897954-87-5

Printed and bound in Spain